LIVING THE FIVE

PARTICIPANT AND LEADER BOOK

JIM AND JENNIFER COWART

Abingdon Press™
Nashville

LIVING THE FIVE:
PARTICIPANT AND LEADER BOOK

This book is printed on acid-free paper.

ISBN: 978-1-5018-2509-5
DVD ISBN: 978-1-5018-2511-8
Streaming Video 1 ISBN: 978-1-5018-2512-5
Streaming Video 2 ISBN: 978-1-5018-2513-2
Streaming Video 3 ISBN: 978-1-5018-2514-9
Streaming Video 4 ISBN: 978-1-5018-2515-6
Streaming Video 5 ISBN: 978-1-5018-2516-3

Our appreciation goes to Rick Warren and Saddleback Church for their work in defining the five
purposes and to New Spring Church in formation of the slogans.

16 17 18 19 20 21 22 23 24 25—10 9 8 7 6 5 4 3 2 1
MANUFACTURED IN THE UNITED STATES OF AMERICA

CONTENTS

APPENDICES

COMMUNITY GROUP LEADERS

FOREWORD

BY RICK WARREN

Jim and Jen Cowart planted a church in 2001, and I watched this church every year grow stronger, grow deeper, grow healthier, grow larger, and grow more visionary. In fact, this church is one of Saddleback's Church Health Award winners! We are pretty picky about the churches that we honor because they must be balanced in worship, in fellowship, in discipleship, in ministry, and in evangelism. They are doing the purposes of God through the processes that balance all of these things. They have the strategy and the structure that allow them to grow year after year after year.

What does it mean to be purpose driven?

We believe, and the Bible teaches in Acts 2, John 17, Ephesians 4, and other places, that God wants your church to be built around God's eternal purposes. There are five of those purposes—not four, not six, not seven. They are modeled by the church in Acts 2; they are prayed for by Jesus in John 17; they are explained by Paul in Ephesians 4; but they are best seen in the Great Commandment and the Great Commission. We believe that a great commitment to the Great Commandment and the Great Commission will grow a great church. This is no theory, friend; this works. We've seen it work in rural areas, urban areas, and suburban areas, and regardless of the size or the denomination of your church, you can be built around the purposes of God.

INTRODUCTION

WELCOME TO LIVING THE FIVE!

Whether you've been a Christ follower for years or you're just checking out the Christian faith for the very first time—welcome! This five-week study is designed to give you new insights into the Bible, how it applies to us, and what it looks like to live it out.

Each week you'll have opportunities to share your own ideas and experiences, watch a short video teaching on that week's theme, discuss the scriptures, learn from each other, and build relationships with others in your group. There's also lots of extra material if you want to really dig in, including options for further study and questions for life application.

At the end of each session, you will find daily devotions that will allow you to slow down and reflect on God's promises and precepts. You will then have a chance to respond by journaling. By doing this study, you'll be learning with a large group in church, a small group in a living room, and alone with God on your own.

We're excited about what God has in store for you and your group over the next five weeks, and we're praying that you will experience God in a fresh way as a result of this study.

JIM AND JENNIFER COWART

TOOLS TO HELP YOU HAVE A GREAT COMMUNITY GROUP EXPERIENCE

1. Notice in the table of contents that there are three sections: (1) Sessions, (2) Appendices, and (3) Community Group Leaders. Familiarize yourself with the appendices. Some of them will be used in the sessions themselves.

2. If you are facilitating/leading or coleading a community group, the Community Group Leaders section will give you some proven experiences from others that will encourage you and help you avoid many common obstacles to effective community group leadership.

3. Use this workbook as a guide, not a straightjacket. If the group responds to the lesson in an unexpected but honest way, go with that. If you think of a better question than the next one in the lesson, ask it. Take to heart the insights included in the Frequent Questions pages and the Community Group Leaders section.

4. Enjoy your community group experience and have fun together.

5. Pray before each session—for your group members, for your time together, and for wisdom and insights.

6. Read the Outline of Each Session on the next pages so you understand how the sessions will flow.

OUTLINE OF EACH SESSION

A TYPICAL GROUP SESSION FOR THE LIVING THE FIVE STUDY WILL INCLUDE THE FOLLOWING SECTIONS. READ THROUGH THIS TO GET A CLEAR IDEA OF HOW EACH GROUP MEETING WILL BE STRUCTURED.

WEEKLY MEMORY VERSES

Each session opens with a memory verse that emphasizes an important truth from the session. This is an optional exercise, but we believe that memorizing scripture can be a vital part of filling our minds with God's will for our lives. We encourage you to give this important habit a try. The verses for our five sessions are also listed in the appendix.

INTRODUCTION

Each lesson opens with a brief thought that will help you prepare for the session and get you thinking about the particular subject you will explore with your group. Make it a practice to read these before the session. You may want to have the group read them out loud.

SHARE YOUR STORY

The foundation for spiritual growth is an intimate connection with God and God's people. You build that connection by sharing your story with a few people who really know you and who earn your trust. This section includes some simple questions to get you talking—letting you share as much or as little of your story as you feel comfortable doing. Each session typically offers you two options. You can get to know your whole group by using the icebreaker question(s), or you can check in with one or two group members for a deeper connection and encouragement in your spiritual journey.

HEAR GOD'S STORY

In this section, you'll read the Bible and listen to teaching in order to hear God's story and begin to see how God's story aligns with yours. When

the study directs, you'll pop in the DVD and watch a short teaching segment. You'll then have an opportunity to read a passage of scripture, and discuss both the teaching and the text. You won't focus on accumulating information but on how you should live in light of God's word. We help you apply the insights from scripture practically and creatively—from your heart as well as your head. At the end of the day, allowing the timeless truths from God's word to transform our lives in Christ should be your greatest aim.

STUDY NOTES

This brief section provides additional commentary, background, or insights on the passage you'll study in the Hear God's Story section.

CREATE A NEW STORY

God wants you to be a part of his kingdom—to weave your story into the divine story. That will mean change. It will require you to go God's way rather than your own. This won't happen overnight, but it should happen steadily. By making small, simple choices, we can begin to change our direction. This is where the Bible's instructions to "be doers of the word and not only hearers" (James 1:22 CEB) comes into play. Many people skip over this aspect of the Christian life because it's scary, relationally awkward, or simply too much work for their busy schedules. But Jesus wanted all of the disciples to know him personally, carry out his commands, and help outsiders connect with him. This doesn't necessarily mean preaching on street corners. It could mean welcoming newcomers, hosting a short-term group in

your home, or walking through this study with a friend. In this study, you'll have an opportunity to go beyond Bible study to a shared Christian life. This section will also have a question or two that will challenge you to live out your faith by serving others, sharing your faith, and worshipping God.

DIGGING DEEPER

If you have time and want to dig deeper into more Bible passages about the topic at hand, we've provided additional passages and questions, which you can use either during the meeting or as homework. Your group may choose to read and prepare before each meeting in order to cover more biblical material. Or group members can use the additional study section during the week after the meeting. If you prefer not to do study homework, this section will provide you with plenty to discuss within the group. These options allow individuals or the whole group to expand their study while still accommodating those who can't do homework or are new to your group.

DAILY DEVOTIONS

Each week on the Daily Devotions pages, we provide scriptures to read and reflect on between sessions—a month's worth of reflections to keep God's word near your heart. This provides you with a chance to slow down, read just a small portion of scripture each day, and reflect and pray through it. You'll then have a chance to journal your response to what you've read. Use this section to seek God on your own throughout the week. This time at home should begin and end with prayer. Don't get in a hurry; take enough time to hear God's direction.

YOU CAN'T DO LIFE

ALONE

One of the first things Jesus did when he began his earthly ministry was recruit a ragtag bunch of fishermen, tax collectors, and others to hang out with him. These ordinary people went on to do extraordinary things as Jesus's disciples, but in the beginning they were simply Jesus's friends and, in a way, his small group.

If Jesus needed to walk through life with other people, we definitely do. Yet so often we isolate ourselves, leaving ourselves open to temptation, loneliness, and all kinds of negative influences and bad decisions. We're stronger when we're not alone. God created us to need each other as we live out our commitment to Jesus.

Not only that, doing life together is just more fun! As we build relationships with other Christ-followers, we can encourage each other, pray for each other, laugh together, and learn together. Christian music artist Sara Groves says these relationships make life "half as hard and twice as good."* That's what we want for each one of you, in this community group and in our church, and it's the focus of today's session.

IF JESUS NEEDED TO WALK THROUGH LIFE WITH OTHER PEOPLE, WE DEFINITELY DO.

* Sara Groves, vocal performance of "Twice as Good," by Christa Wells and Sara Groves, recorded on *Fireflies and Songs*, released 2009, Kiss Me Not Publishing and Sara Groves Musics.

SHARE YOUR STORY

EACH OF US HAS A STORY. THE EVENTS OF OUR LIVES—GOOD, BAD, WONDERFUL, OR CHALLENGING—HAVE SHAPED WHO WE ARE.

GOD KNOWS YOUR STORY, AND GOD INTENDS TO REDEEM IT—TO USE EVERY STRUGGLE AND EVERY JOY TO ULTIMATELY BRING YOU INTO RELATIONSHIP WITH GOD. WHEN WE SHARE OUR STORIES WITH OTHERS, WE GIVE THEM THE OPPORTUNITY TO SEE GOD AT WORK.

WHEN WE SHARE OUR STORIES, WE ALSO REALIZE WE ARE NOT ALONE—THAT WE HAVE COMMON EXPERIENCES AND THOUGHTS AND THAT OTHERS CAN UNDERSTAND WHAT WE ARE GOING THROUGH. YOUR STORY CAN ENCOURAGE SOMEONE ELSE. AND TELLING IT CAN LEAD TO A PATH OF FREEDOM FOR YOU AND FOR THOSE YOU SHARE IT WITH.

- Open your group with prayer. This should be a brief, simple prayer in which you invite God to give you insight as you study. You can pray for specific requests at the end of the meeting, or stop momentarily to pray if a particular situation comes up during your discussion.

- Before you start this first meeting, get contact information for every participant. Take time to pass around a copy of the Community Group Roster on page 86, a sheet of paper, or your personal Participant Guide, opened to the Community Group Roster. Ask someone to make copies or type up a list with everyone's information and e-mail it to the group during the week.

1. **WHAT BROUGHT YOU HERE? WHAT DO YOU HOPE TO GET OUT OF THIS GROUP?**

2. **WHAT'S YOUR USUAL APPROACH TO MEETING NEW PEOPLE?**
   A. **TO BE HONEST, IT'S PRETTY SCARY FOR ME.**
   B. **I'M CAUTIOUS AT FIRST, BUT WHEN I FEEL COMFORTABLE I OPEN UP.**
   C. **I'VE NEVER REALLY MET A STRANGER—WHAT DO YOU WANT TO KNOW?!**

Whether your group is new or ongoing, it's always important to reflect on and review your values together. On page 83 is a Community Group Covenant with the values we've found most useful in sustaining healthy, balanced groups. We recommend that you choose one or two values— ones you haven't previously focused on or have room to grow in—to emphasize during this study. Choose ones that will take your group to the next stage of intimacy and spiritual health.

We recommend you rotate host homes on a regular basis and let the hosts lead the meeting. Studies show that healthy groups rotate leadership. This helps to develop every member's ability to shepherd a few people in a safe environment. Even Jesus gave others the opportunity to serve alongside him (Mark 6:30-44). Look at the Frequent Questions in the appendix for additional information about hosting or leading the group.

TAKE TIME TO GET TO KNOW EACH OTHER. INTRODUCE EVERYONE—YOU MAY EVEN WANT TO HAVE NAME TAGS FOR YOUR FIRST MEETING.

The Community Group Calendar on page 85 is a tool for planning who will host and lead each meeting. Take a few minutes to plan hosts and leaders for your remaining meetings. Don't skip this important step! It will revolutionize your group.

WATCH
THE DVD

- Write down key thoughts, questions, and things you want to remember or talk about together.

- After watching the video, have someone read the discussion questions in the Hear God's Story section and direct the discussion among the group.

- As you go through each of the subsequent sections, ask someone else to read the questions and direct the discussion.

HEAR GOD'S STORY

SOME PEOPLE THINK "EMOTION WILL SUSTAIN DEVOTION"— THAT CHRISTIANITY IS A MATTER OF MOVING FROM ONE SPIRITUAL HIGH TO THE NEXT AND THAT IF YOU CAN SUSTAIN THESE FEELINGS IT WILL BE EASY TO FOLLOW CHRIST.

UNFORTUNATELY, LIFE IS SOMETIMES HARD, AND IT'S UNREALISTIC TO EXPECT YOUR EMOTIONS TO DRIVE YOUR SPIRITUAL LIFE. INSTEAD, YOU NEED TO BE GROUNDED IN GOD'S WORD, IN DAILY COMMUNICATION WITH GOD IN PRAYER, AND IN CONNECTION TO OTHER BELIEVERS WHO CAN STRENGTHEN YOUR FAITH. LIFE IS FULL OF MOUNTAINS AND VALLEYS, BUT GOD DESIGNED US TO TRAVEL THE PATH TOGETHER.

READ 1 SAMUEL 20:12-13, 16-17

*Then Jonathan told David, "I pledge by the L*ORD *God of Israel that I will question my father by this time tomorrow or on the third day. If he seems favorable toward David, I will definitely send word and make sure you know. But if my father intends to harm you, then may the L*ORD *deal harshly with me, Jonathan, and worse still if I don't tell you right away so that you can escape safely. May the L*ORD *be with you as he once was with my father. . . .*

*"If Jonathan's name is also eliminated, then the L*ORD *will seek retribution from David!" So Jonathan again made a pledge to David because he loved David as much as himself (CEB).*

1. **WHY DO YOU THINK JONATHAN WAS SO WILLING TO HELP DAVID, EVEN AT A COST TO HIMSELF?**

2. **HOW HAD THE LORD BEEN WITH JONATHAN'S FATHER, SAUL?**

3. **JONATHAN'S STATEMENT IN VERSE 16 IMPLICATES SAUL AS ONE OF DAVID'S ENEMIES. WHY WOULD JONATHAN MAKE A SOLEMN PLEDGE AGAINST HIS OWN FATHER?**

4. **IN ANCIENT CULTURES, IF BOTH PARTIES REPEATED THE TERMS IT MADE A SOLEMN PLEDGE UNBREAKABLE. WHAT INSIGHT DOES THIS GIVE YOU INTO VERSE 17?**

STUDY NOTES

IN THE VIDEO, JIM AND JENNIFER QUOTED HEBREWS 10:24, WHICH SAYS WE ARE TO "SPUR" ONE ANOTHER ON (NIV).

EVEN IF YOU'VE NEVER RIDDEN A HORSE, YOU'RE PROBABLY FAMILIAR WITH SPURS FROM THE MOVIES. BASICALLY THEY ARE JUST SMALL METAL TOOLS A RIDER WEARS ON HIS OR HER BOOTS, AND WHEN THE RIDER WANTS TO URGE THE HORSE TO WALK OR RUN MORE QUICKLY OR MOVE FROM SIDE TO SIDE, HE OR SHE GENTLY PUSHES THE SPUR INTO THE HORSE'S SIDE.

WHEN USED CORRECTLY A SPUR DOES NOT HURT THE HORSE, BUT IT CAN BE A GREAT WAY TO REINFORCE THE RIDER'S OTHER COMMANDS OR COMMUNICATE QUICKLY AND CLEARLY DURING RIDING.

In addition to the wonderful metaphor of this verse, which gives us a word picture of urging each other on to do better, it's also one of many verses in the Bible you just can't obey if you don't participate in the life of a church and connect with other believers.

HERE ARE A FEW MORE:

Love each other like the members of your family. Be the best at showing honor to each other.
Romans 12:10 (CEB)

Serve each other through love.
Galatians 5:13 (CEB)

Be kind, compassionate, and forgiving to each other, in the same way God forgave you in Christ.
Ephesians 4:32 (CEB)

CREATE A NEW STORY

GOD WANTS YOU TO BE PART OF GOD'S KINGDOM—TO WEAVE YOUR STORY INTO GOD'S.

THAT WILL MEAN CHANGE—TO GO GOD'S WAY RATHER THAN YOUR OWN. THIS WON'T HAPPEN OVERNIGHT, BUT IT SHOULD HAPPEN STEADILY. BY STARTING WITH SMALL, SIMPLE CHOICES, WE BEGIN TO CHANGE OUR DIRECTION.

THE HOLY SPIRIT HELPS US ALONG THE WAY—GIVING US GIFTS TO SERVE THE BODY, OFFERING US INSIGHTS INTO SCRIPTURE, AND CHALLENGING US TO LOVE NOT ONLY THOSE AROUND US BUT THOSE FAR FROM GOD.

IN THIS SECTION, TALK ABOUT HOW YOU WILL APPLY THE WISDOM YOU'VE LEARNED FROM THE TEACHING AND BIBLE STUDY. THEN THINK ABOUT PRACTICAL STEPS YOU CAN TAKE IN THE COMING WEEK TO LIVE OUT WHAT YOU'VE LEARNED.

1. HAVE YOU EVER MADE BAD DECISIONS WHEN YOU WERE ALONE? HOW WOULD THE PRESENCE OF OTHER PEOPLE WHO CARED ABOUT YOU POTENTIALLY HAVE MADE A DIFFERENCE IN THOSE SITUATIONS?

2. IS IT INTIMIDATING OR SCARY TO THINK OF LETTING YOUR GROUP GET TO KNOW THE REAL YOU?

3. HAVE YOU ISOLATED YOURSELF IN ANY AREA OF LIFE? WHAT STEPS CAN YOU TAKE TO BEGIN SHARING THAT PART OF YOUR LIFE WITH OTHERS?

4. WHAT ARE SOME CONCRETE WAYS YOU CAN SPUR EACH OTHER ON THIS WEEK?

5. TAKE A LOOK AT THE SEGMENTS BELOW AND WRITE THE NAMES OF TWO OR THREE PEOPLE YOU KNOW. COMMIT TO PRAYING FOR GOD'S GUIDANCE AND AN OPPORTUNITY TO SHARE WITH EACH OF THEM. PERHAPS THEY WOULD BE OPEN TO JOINING THE GROUP? SHARE YOUR LISTS WITH THE GROUP SO YOU CAN ALL BE PRAYING FOR THE PEOPLE YOU'VE IDENTIFIED.

FAMILY (immediate or extended)	
FAMILIAR (neighbors, kids' sports teams, school, and so forth)	
FRIENDS	
FUN (gym, hobbies, hangouts)	
FIRM (work)	

6. CONSIDER SOMEONE—IN THIS GROUP OR OUTSIDE IT—THAT YOU CAN BEGIN GOING DEEPER WITH IN AN INTENTIONAL WAY. THIS MIGHT BE YOUR MOM OR DAD, A COUSIN, AN AUNT OR UNCLE, A ROOMMATE, A COLLEGE BUDDY, OR A NEIGHBOR. CHOOSE SOMEONE WHO MIGHT BE OPEN TO "DOING LIFE" WITH YOU AT A DEEPER LEVEL, AND PRAY ABOUT THAT OPPORTUNITY.

7. THIS WEEK, HOW WILL YOU INTERACT WITH THE BIBLE? CAN YOU COMMIT TO SPENDING TIME IN DAILY PRAYER OR STUDY OF GOD'S WORD (USE THE DAILY DEVOTIONS SECTION TO GUIDE YOU)? TELL THE GROUP HOW YOU PLAN TO FOLLOW JESUS THIS WEEK, AND THEN, AT YOUR NEXT MEETING, TALK ABOUT YOUR PROGRESS AND CHALLENGES.

8. STACK YOUR HANDS (LIKE A SPORTS TEAM DOES IN THE HUDDLE) AND COMMIT TO TAKING A RISK AND GOING DEEPER IN YOUR GROUP AND IN YOUR RELATIONSHIPS WITH EACH OTHER.

9. TO CLOSE YOUR TIME TOGETHER, SPEND SOME TIME WORSHIPPING GOD TOGETHER—PRAYING, SINGING, READING SCRIPTURE.

- Have someone use his or her musical gifts to lead the group in a worship song. Try singing a cappella, using a worship CD, or having someone accompany your singing with a musical instrument.

- Choose a psalm or other favorite verse, and read it aloud together. Make it a time of praise and worship, as the words remind you of all God has done for you.

- Ask, "How can we pray for you this week?" Invite everyone to share, but don't force the issue. Be sure to write prayer requests on your Prayer Requests and Praise Reports (page 87).

- Close your meeting with prayer.

DIGGING DEEPER

IF YOU FEEL GOD NUDGING YOU TO GO DEEPER, TAKE SOME TIME BEFORE THE NEXT MEETING TO DIG INTO GOD'S WORD.

EXPLORE THE BIBLE PASSAGES RELATED TO THIS SESSION'S THEME ON YOUR OWN, AND JOT YOUR REFLECTIONS IN A JOURNAL OR IN THIS STUDY GUIDE.

A GREAT WAY TO GAIN INSIGHT ON A PASSAGE IS TO READ IT IN SEVERAL DIFFERENT TRANSLATIONS.

YOU MAY WANT TO USE A BIBLE APP OR WEBSITE TO COMPARE TRANSLATIONS.

READ JOHN 15:12-17

1. WE WILL PROBABLY NEVER BE REQUIRED TO PHYSICALLY DIE FOR A FRIEND. WHAT ELSE COULD JESUS MEAN WHEN HE CALLS US TO LAY DOWN OUR LIVES FOR EACH OTHER?

2. JESUS TELLS HIS DISCIPLES TWICE TO LOVE EACH OTHER. IN THE MIDDLE OF THOSE TWO COMMANDS HE REMINDS THEM TO OBEY AND DO WHAT HE'S ASKED. WHAT'S THE CONNECTION BETWEEN THE TWO?

3. WHAT ARE SOME OF THE THINGS JESUS LEARNED FROM THE FATHER THAT HE PASSED ALONG TO HIS FOLLOWERS?

READ ROMANS 12:9-21

1. THIS PASSAGE IS FULL OF INSTRUCTIONS FOR LIVING IN COMMUNITY WITH OTHER BELIEVERS. WHICH ONE DO YOU FIND MOST CHALLENGING?

2. WHAT DOES VERSE 11 TELL US IS THE KEY TO KEEPING OUR SPIRITUAL FERVOR?

3. WHAT ARE SOME WAYS WE CAN REJOICE WITH THOSE WHO REJOICE? MOURN WITH THOSE WHO MOURN?

DAILY DEVOTIONALS

DAY 1 • READ PROVERBS 13:20

Walk with wise people and become wise; befriend fools and get in trouble (CEB).

RESPOND

How do we grow in wisdom just by associating with other wise people? Why is the opposite also true?

DAY 2 • READ ROMANS 15:7

So welcome each other, in the same way that Christ also welcomed you, for God's glory (CEB).

RESPOND

What are some ways Christ accepted you? How can you show that same acceptance to others?

DAY 3 • READ ECCLESIASTES 4:9-10

Two are better than one because they have a good return for their hard work. If either should fall, one can pick up the other. But how miserable are those who fall and don't have a companion to help them up! (CEB).

RESPOND

Have you ever "fallen" and needed a friend's help? How could you be that friend to someone else? Ask God for opportunities to love other people this way.

DAY 4 • READ PHILIPPIANS 2:1-2

Therefore, if there is any encouragement in Christ, any comfort in love, any sharing in the Spirit, any sympathy, complete my joy by thinking the same way, having the same love, being united, and agreeing with each other (CEB).

RESPOND

Do people always have to agree? How does the rest of the scripture passage explain this command?

DAY 5 • READ 1 JOHN 3:18

Little children, let's not love with words or speech but with action and truth (CEB).

RESPOND

What is the difference between these two kinds of love? How can we love with actions and truth?

DAY 6

Use the following space to write any thoughts God has put in your heart and mind about the things we have looked at in this session and during your Daily Devotions time this week.

_____

_____

_____

_____

_____

GROWING PEOPLE CHANGE

Jesus used many farming metaphors to teach the people of his day: He talked about the seed of the gospel falling on rocky soil and good soil; he described himself as the vine and his people as branches that must remain in him; and he said the potential "harvest" of new believers is plentiful if we will share the good news with them.

In his letters to the early churches, Paul also used agricultural ideas: He wrote that we reap what we sow; he talked about planting and watering new congregations; and in the book of Galatians, he said growing Christians should be like healthy trees, producing fruit as evidence of their growth.

Paul knew a thing or two about growth—he started out as an enemy of the church and was transformed by a dramatic encounter with Christ. His life is a beautiful example of our second principle: growing people change.

GROWING CHRISTIANS SHOULD BE LIKE HEALTHY TREES, PRODUCING FRUIT AS EVIDENCE OF THEIR GROWTH.

SHARE YOUR STORY

AS WE SAID LAST WEEK, WHEN WE SHARE OUR STORIES WITH OTHERS, WE GIVE THEM THE OPPORTUNITY TO SEE GOD AT WORK. YOUR STORY IS BEING SHAPED—EVEN IN THIS MOMENT—BY BEING PART OF THIS GROUP. IN FACT, FEW THINGS CAN SHAPE US MORE THAN COMMUNITY.

WHEN WE SHARE OUR STORIES, WE CAN ENCOURAGE SOMEONE ELSE, AND LEARN. WE EXPERIENCE THE PRESENCE OF GOD AS GOD HELPS US BE BRAVE ENOUGH TO REVEAL OUR THOUGHTS AND FEELINGS.

- Open your group with prayer. This should be a brief, simple prayer, in which you invite God to be with you as you meet. You can pray for specific requests at the end of the meeting, or stop momentarily to pray if a particular situation comes up during your discussion.

1. WHAT'S YOUR SPIRITUAL "PEDIGREE"? HAVE YOU BEEN A CHRISTIAN FOR YEARS? IS FAITH BRAND-NEW FOR YOU? ARE YOU STILL JUST CHECKING OUT CHRISTIANITY?

2. HOW DO YOU KNOW IF YOU'RE GROWING AS A CHRISTIAN?

3. IN THE LAST SESSION WE ASKED YOU TO WRITE SOME NAMES IN THE DIAGRAM. WHO DID YOU IDENTIFY AS THE PEOPLE IN YOUR LIFE WHO NEED TO MEET JESUS? GO BACK TO THE DIAGRAM ON PAGE 11 TO HELP YOU THINK OF VARIOUS PEOPLE WITH WHOM YOU COME IN CONTACT ON A REGULAR BASIS—PEOPLE WHO NEED TO KNOW JESUS MORE DEEPLY. CONSIDER IDEAS FOR ACTION AND MAKE A PLAN TO FOLLOW THROUGH ON ONE OF THEM THIS WEEK.

4. PAIR UP WITH SOMEONE IN YOUR GROUP. (WE SUGGEST THAT MEN PARTNER WITH MEN AND WOMEN WITH WOMEN.) HE OR SHE DOESN'T HAVE TO BE YOUR BEST FRIEND. INSTEAD, THIS PERSON WILL SIMPLY ENCOURAGE YOU TO COMPLETE THE GOALS YOU SET FOR YOURSELF DURING THIS STUDY. FOLLOWING THROUGH ON A RESOLUTION IS TOUGH WHEN YOU'RE ON YOUR OWN; IT MAKES ALL THE DIFFERENCE TO HAVE A PARTNER TO CHEER YOU ON.

WATCH
THE DVD

Watch the DVD for this session now. Use the space provided below to record key thoughts, questions, and things you want to remember or follow up on. After you finish watching the video, have someone read the discussion questions in the Hear God's Story section and direct the discussion among the group. As you go through each of the subsequent sections, ask someone else to read the questions and direct the discussion.

_____

_____

_____

_____

_____

_____

HEAR GOD'S STORY

HOW CAN WE
BECOME PART OF
GOD'S STORY? BY
ALIGNING OUR
STORIES WITH
GOD'S STORY AND
UNDERSTANDING
WHAT IT MEANS TO
FOLLOW GOD. USE
THE FOLLOWING
QUESTIONS,
STORIES YOU JUST
EXPERIENCED, AND
THE BIBLE PASSAGE
ON THE FOLLOWING
PAGE TO GUIDE
YOUR DISCUSSION
OF THE TEACHING.

READ PHILIPPIANS 3:4-8

If anyone else has reason to put their confidence in physical advantages, I have even more: I was circumcised on the eighth day. I am from the people of Israel and the tribe of Benjamin. I am a Hebrew of the Hebrews. With respect to observing the Law, I'm a Pharisee. With respect to devotion to the faith, I harassed the church. With respect to righteousness under the Law, I'm blameless.

These things were my assets, but I wrote them off as a loss for the sake of Christ. But even beyond that, I consider everything a loss in comparison with the superior value of knowing Christ Jesus my Lord. I have lost everything for him, but what I lost I think of as sewer trash, so that I might gain Christ (CEB).

1. **WHAT DOES IT MEAN TO HAVE CONFIDENCE IN YOUR "PHYSICAL ADVANTAGES"?**

2. **WHY DID PAUL LIST ALL HIS ACHIEVEMENTS AND ASSETS? HOW MIGHT THIS HAVE AFFECTED HIS READERS?**

3. **HOW WOULD PAUL'S RELIGIOUS ACCOMPLISHMENTS HAVE PROFITED HIM? WHY WOULD HE NOW CONSIDER THEM TO BE A LOSS?**

4. **THE PHARISEES WERE AN ELITE SECT OF JUDAISM; THEIR NAME MEANS "THE SEPARATED ONES." HOW DO THESE VERSES SHOW PAUL'S TRANSFORMATION FROM PHARISEE TO CHRIST FOLLOWER?**

5. **WHAT IS THE SIGNIFICANCE OF PAUL'S COMMENT THAT HE WROTE OFF HIS ASSETS AS A LOSS? WERE THEY WRONG IN THEMSELVES?**

STUDY NOTES

IF YOU'RE NOT FAMILIAR WITH THE JEWISH TRADITION AND THE STORY OF THE ISRAELITES IN THE OLD TESTAMENT, PAUL'S WORDS IN PHILIPPIANS 3 CAN BE CONFUSING. WHY IS HE TALKING ABOUT CIRCUMCISION? WHY DOES IT MATTER WHAT TRIBE HE CAME FROM?

CIRCUMCISED: BEGINNING WITH ABRAHAM, GOD COMMANDS THE MALES AMONG GOD'S CHOSEN PEOPLE, THE ISRAELITES, TO BE CIRCUMCISED EIGHT DAYS AFTER BIRTH. NOW, AS THE NON-JEWISH (GENTILE) PEOPLE BEGIN BELIEVING IN JESUS AND JOINING THE CHURCH, SOME OF THE JEWS THINK GENTILES SHOULD BE CIRCUMCISED TOO. PAUL IS DISPUTING THIS ATTITUDE AND USING HIS OWN CREDENTIALS AS A FAITHFUL "LIFETIME" JEW TO DO SO.

FROM THE PEOPLE OF ISRAEL AND THE TRIBE OF BENJAMIN: PAUL CAN TRACE HIS SPIRITUAL LINEAGE ALL THE WAY BACK TO THE ESTABLISHMENT OF THE ORIGINAL TWELVE TRIBES OF ISRAEL. BENJAMIN WAS A FAVORED TRIBE AND PRODUCED THE FIRST KING OF ISRAEL, SAUL, WHO BRIEFLY ENTERED OUR STORY LAST WEEK. IT'S POSSIBLE SAUL/PAUL WAS EVEN NAMED AFTER HIM. AGAIN, PAUL IS SAYING THAT IF ANYONE HAS REASON TO BOAST IN SUCH THINGS, IT'S HIM—BUT HE'S NOT BOASTING BECAUSE KNOWING CHRIST IS MORE IMPORTANT.

WITH RESPECT TO DEVOTION . . . I HARASSED THE CHURCH: IN GALATIANS 1:13, PAUL SAYS, "YOU HEARD ABOUT MY PREVIOUS LIFE IN JUDAISM, HOW SEVERELY I HARASSED GOD'S CHURCH AND TRIED TO DESTROY IT" (CEB). HIS "CREDENTIALS" IN THIS AREA WERE WELL-KNOWN.

CREATE A NEW STORY

IN THIS SECTION, TALK ABOUT HOW YOU WILL APPLY THE WISDOM YOU'VE LEARNED FROM THE TEACHING AND BIBLE STUDY.

THEN THINK ABOUT PRACTICAL STEPS YOU CAN TAKE IN THE COMING WEEK TO LIVE OUT WHAT YOU'VE LEARNED.

1. ON THE VIDEO, JIM AND JENNIFER GIVE SEVERAL NEXT STEPS YOU CAN TAKE TO GROW SPIRITUALLY. WHICH ONES DO YOU NEED TO MAKE PART OF YOUR LIFE?

2. HAVE YOU EVER EXPERIENCED THE BIBLE BEING A LIGHT FOR YOUR PATH AND GIVING YOU DIRECTION FOR LIFE?

3. WHY IS BAPTISM SO IMPORTANT?

4. JIM AND JENNIFER SAY THAT A CHANGED HEART IS KEY TO LIFE CHANGE, BECAUSE UNLESS YOU CAN ADMIT THE WAYS YOU NEED TO GROW, THE PROCESS WILL NEVER START. ARE THERE THINGS YOU NEED TO CHANGE IN YOUR HEART AND LIFE?

5. HAVE YOU EVER SHARED YOUR FAITH WITH SOMEONE ELSE? HOW DID THAT EXPERIENCE GO?

6. HERE ARE SOME SIMPLE WAYS TO CONNECT WITH GOD. TELL THE GROUP WHICH ONES YOU PLAN TO TRY THIS WEEK, AND TALK ABOUT YOUR PROGRESS AND CHALLENGES WHEN YOU MEET NEXT TIME.

- Pray. Commit to personal prayer and daily connection with God. You may find it helpful to write your prayers in a journal.

- Daily Devotions. The Daily Devotions provided in each session offer an opportunity to read a short Bible passage five days a week during the course of our study. In our hurry-up world, we often move too quickly through everything—even reading God's word! Slow down. Don't just skim, but take time to read carefully and reflect on the passage. Write down your insights on what you read each day. Copy a portion of scripture on a card and tape it somewhere in your line of sight, such as your car's dashboard or the bathroom mirror. Or text it to yourself! Think about it when you sit at red lights or while you're eating a meal. Reflect on what God is saying to you through these words. On the sixth day summarize what God has shown you throughout the week.

7. TO CLOSE YOUR TIME TOGETHER, SPEND SOME TIME WORSHIPPING GOD TOGETHER—PRAYING, SINGING, OR READING SCRIPTURE.

- Have someone use his or her musical gifts to lead the group in a worship song. Try singing a cappella, using a worship CD, or having someone accompany your singing with a musical instrument.

- Choose a psalm or other favorite verse and read it aloud together. Make it a time of praise and worship as the words remind you of all God has done for you.

- Ask, "How can we pray for you this week?" Invite everyone to share, but don't force the issue. Be sure to write prayer requests on your Prayer Requests and Praise Reports on page 87.

- Close your meeting with prayer.

DIGGING DEEPER

IF YOU FEEL GOD IS
NUDGING YOU TO
GO DEEPER, TAKE
SOME TIME BETWEEN
NOW AND OUR NEXT
MEETING TO DIG INTO
GOD'S WORD. EXPLORE
THE BIBLE PASSAGES
RELATED TO THIS
SESSION'S THEME ON
YOUR OWN, JOTTING
YOUR REFLECTIONS
IN A JOURNAL OR IN
THIS PARTICIPANT
GUIDE. WANT TO GO
DEEPER? SELECT A
FEW VERSES AND TRY
PARAPHRASING THEM—
WRITING THEM IN YOUR
OWN WORDS. IF YOU
LIKE, SHARE THEM WITH
THE GROUP THE NEXT
TIME YOU MEET.

READ JAMES 1:2-4

1. **TRIALS AND STRUGGLES ARE ONE WAY GOD OFTEN FORCES US TO GROW. WHY DOES JAMES SAY WE SHOULD WELCOME THESE EXPERIENCES?**

2. **WHY IS ENDURANCE A RESULT OF OUR FAITH BEING TESTED?**

3. **WHAT DOES IT MEAN TO "LET . . . ENDURANCE COMPLETE ITS WORK"?**

READ GALATIANS 5:22-25

1. IS THE SPIRIT PRODUCING ANY OF THIS FRUIT IN YOUR LIFE RIGHT NOW? ARE THERE ANY YOU WANT GOD TO DEVELOP IN YOU?

2. WHAT DOES IT MEAN TO CRUCIFY YOUR "SELF WITH ITS PASSIONS AND ITS DESIRES"?

3. HOW DO WE KEEP IN STEP WITH THE SPIRIT?

DAILY DEVOTIONALS

DAY 1 • READ MATTHEW 7:16-18

Do people get bunches of grapes from thorny weeds, or do they get figs from thistles? In the same way, every good tree produces good fruit, and every rotten tree produces bad fruit. A good tree can't produce bad fruit. And a rotten tree can't produce good fruit (CEB).

RESPOND

Consider verse 18. Based on your own experience, do you find this to be true?

DAY 2 • READ 1 PETER 2:2-3

Instead, like a newborn baby, desire the pure milk of the word. Nourished by it, you will grow into salvation, since you have tasted that the Lord is good (CEB).

RESPOND

What are examples of the "milk" that can help people grow? Do you need any of them in your life? Give thanks for the ways they have shown you the Lord is good.

DAY 3 • READ EPHESIANS 4:15-16

Instead, by speaking the truth with love, let's grow in every way into Christ, who is the head. The whole body grows from him, as it is joined and held together by all the supporting ligaments. The body makes itself grow in that it builds itself up with love as each one does its part (CEB).

RESPOND

These verses remind us we have a responsibility not only for our own growth but for the growth of our fellow believers. It doesn't work for one part of the body to grow and none of the rest! How can you help others grow and change?

DAY 4 • READ COLOSSIANS 2:6-7

So live in Christ Jesus the Lord in the same way as you recieved him. Be rooted and built up in him, be established in faith, and overflow with thanksgiving just as you were taught (CEB).

RESPOND

What does it mean to be "rooted" in Christ? Does this describe your life?

DAY 5 • READ PSALM 92:12-13

The righteous will spring up like a palm tree. / They will grow strong like a cedar of Lebanon. / Those who have been replanted in the Lord's house / will spring up in the courtyards of our God (CEB).

RESPOND

Ask God to help you apply what you've learned this week, and ask for wisdom about how you can grow more deeply and flourish in your faith.

DAY 6

Use the following space to write any thoughts God has put in your heart and mind about the things we have looked at in this session and during your Daily Devotions time this week.

_____

_____

_____

Saved PEOPLE Serve PEOPLE

Some people are slaves to their work or to their addictions or to their egos. We all choose how we're going to invest our time, our energy, and even our money, and no one is exempt from being a servant to something.

Fortunately, as Christians we don't have to be captive to these things. We are created to serve God and to serve other people, and throughout scripture we see this is actually a way to not only grow spiritually but to experience deep joy and meaning in life. Christianity is not a cruise ship where it's all about us; it's a disciple-ship, and when you get on board, you're automatically part of the work crew—and part of a fulfilling adventure with Jesus. Saved people serve people, and today we'll explore why this is so foundational to our calling as a church.

WE ARE CREATED TO SERVE GOD AND TO SERVE OTHER PEOPLE.

SHARE YOUR STORY

OPEN YOUR GROUP WITH PRAYER. THIS SHOULD BE A BRIEF, SIMPLE PRAYER IN WHICH YOU INVITE GOD TO BE WITH YOU AS YOU MEET. YOU CAN PRAY FOR SPECIFIC REQUESTS AT THE END OF THE MEETING OR STOP MOMENTARILY TO PRAY IF A PARTICULAR SITUATION COMES UP DURING YOUR DISCUSSION.

SHARING PERSONAL STORIES BUILDS DEEPER CONNECTIONS AMONG GROUP MEMBERS. BEGIN YOUR TIME TOGETHER BY USING THE FOLLOWING QUESTIONS AND ACTIVITIES TO GET PEOPLE TALKING.

1. Have you ever been part of a service project with a church or a community organization? How did you feel about that experience?

2. Have you ever received great service from a company or business? How did it make you feel?

3. Break into smaller groups, and share your thoughts on serving others.

WATCH
THE DVD

Watch the DVD for this session now. Use the space provided below to record key thoughts, questions, and things you want to remember or follow up on. After you finish watching the video, have someone read the discussion questions in the Hear God's Story section and direct the discussion among the group. As you go through each of the subsequent sections, ask someone else to read the questions and direct the discussion.

_____

_____

_____

_____

_____

_____

_____

HEAR GOD'S STORY

DOES SERVING OTHERS SEEM DEMEANING? IN MATTHEW 20:28, JESUS SAID HE DIDN'T COME TO BE SERVED BUT TO SERVE OTHERS, AND TO GIVE HIS LIFE AWAY FOR US.

READ ACTS 18:24-28

Meanwhile, a certain Jew named Apollos arrived in Ephesus. He was a native of Alexandria and was well-educated and effective in his use of the scriptures. He had been instructed in the way of the Lord and spoke as one stirred up by the Spirit. He taught accurately the things about Jesus, even though he was aware only of the baptism John proclaimed and practiced. He began speaking with confidence in the synagogue. When Priscilla and Aquila heard him, they received him into their circle of friends and explained to him God's way more accurately. When he wanted to travel to Achaia, the brothers and sisters encouraged him and wrote to the disciples so they would open their homes to him. Once he arrived, he was of great help to those who had come to believe through grace. He would vigorously defeat Jewish arguments in public debate, using the scriptures to prove that Jesus was the Christ (CEB).

USE THE FOLLOWING QUESTIONS TO GUIDE YOUR DISCUSSION OF THE TEACHING AND STORIES YOU JUST EXPERIENCED ON THE DVD AND THE BIBLE PASSAGE ABOVE.

1. **WHAT DOES IT MEAN THAT APOLLOS ONLY KNEW ABOUT THE BAPTISM OF JOHN?**

2. **PRISCILLA AND AQUILA COULD HAVE BEEN INTIMIDATED BY APOLLOS BECAUSE HE WAS SUCH A POWERFUL SPEAKER. INSTEAD THEY CHOSE TO MAKE HIM EVEN BETTER. WHAT DOES THIS TEACH US ABOUT SERVING OTHERS?**

3. HOW DOES APOLLOS ALSO DEMONSTRATE A SERVANT'S HEART IN THE ENCOUNTER WITH PRISCILLA AND AQUILA?

4. NOTICE THAT PRISCILLA AND AQUILA ARE MINISTRY PARTNERS, OR COWORKERS. HOW DOES THEIR HOME GROUP SHOW FRIENDS AND GUESTS LIKE APOLLOS HOW TO LIVE MORE FAITHFULLY?

5. READ ROMANS 16:3-5

SHOWING KINDNESS AND HOSPITALITY TO OTHERS IS A FORM OF SERVICE. HAVE YOU EVER THOUGHT ABOUT THESE ACTIONS AS A WAY TO SERVE? WHAT OTHER ATTITUDES OR BEHAVIORS CAN BE WAYS TO SERVE PEOPLE?

Say hello to Prisca [Priscilla] and Aquila, my coworkers in Christ Jesus, who risked their own necks for my life. I'm not the only one who thanks God for them, but all the churches of the Gentiles do the same. Also say hello to the church that meets in their house. Say hello to Epaenetus, my dear friend, who was the first convert in Asia for Christ.
—**Romans 16:3-5 CEB**

STUDY NOTES

ONE OF THE GREATEST EXAMPLES OF JESUS SERVING OTHERS IS FOUND IN JOHN 13. HERE, JESUS GETS DOWN ON HIS HANDS AND KNEES AND WASHES THE FEET OF HIS DISCIPLES. VERSES 3-5 SAY, "JESUS KNEW THE FATHER HAD GIVEN EVERYTHING INTO HIS HANDS AND THAT HE HAD COME FROM GOD AND WAS RETURNING TO GOD. SO HE GOT UP FROM THE TABLE AND TOOK OFF HIS ROBES. PICKING UP A LINEN TOWEL, HE TIED IT AROUND HIS WAIST. THEN HE POURED WATER INTO A WASHBASIN AND BEGAN TO WASH THE DISCIPLES' FEET, DRYING THEM WITH THE TOWEL HE WAS WEARING" (CEB).

In Bible times, people walked a great deal on dusty roads, usually wearing only sandals, and their feet got very dirty. It was an expected part of hospitality that a host would provide water for guests to wash their own feet, but in very wealthy households a slave would perform this service. It was considered one of the most undignified, lowly tasks a servant could do.

Because of this, Jesus's disciples knew their master had just served and honored them in a significant way. But as the story ends, he makes sure they understand how to apply it.

In John 13:12-17, we read, *"After he washed the disciples' feet, he put on his robes and returned to his place at the table. He said to them, 'Do you know what I've done for you? You call me "Teacher" and "Lord," and you speak correctly, because I am. If I, your Lord and teacher, have washed your feet, you too must wash each other's feet. I have given you an example: Just as I have done, you also must do. I assure you, servants aren't greater than their master, nor are those who are sent greater than the one who sent them. Since you know these things, you will be happy if you do them'"* (CEB).

CREATE A NEW STORY

GOD WANTS YOU TO BE PART OF GOD'S KINGDOM—TO WEAVE YOUR STORY INTO GOD'S. THAT WILL MEAN CHANGE. IT WILL REQUIRE YOU TO GO GOD'S WAY RATHER THAN YOUR OWN. THIS WON'T HAPPEN OVERNIGHT, BUT IT SHOULD HAPPEN STEADILY. BY MAKING SMALL, SIMPLE CHOICES, WE CAN BEGIN TO CHANGE OUR DIRECTION. THE HOLY SPIRIT HELPS US ALONG THE WAY BY GIVING US GIFTS TO SERVE THE BODY, OFFERING US INSIGHTS INTO SCRIPTURE, AND CHALLENGING US TO LOVE NOT ONLY THOSE AROUND US BUT THOSE FAR FROM GOD.

IN THIS SECTION, TALK ABOUT HOW YOU WILL APPLY THE WISDOM YOU'VE LEARNED IN THIS SESSION.

1. JIM AND JENNIFER SAY THAT WHEN WE SERVE, WE'RE OFTEN BLESSED AT LEAST AS MUCH AS THE PEOPLE WE'RE SERVING. HAVE YOU EXPERIENCED THIS?

2. HAVE YOU EVER TAKEN A SPIRITUAL GIFTS TEST OR THOUGHT ABOUT YOUR UNIQUE TALENTS? WHAT ABILITIES OR SKILLS DO YOU HAVE THAT COULD BUILD UP THE CHURCH?

3. WHAT DOES SERVING OTHERS TEACH US ABOUT OURSELVES?

4. GROUPS GROW CLOSER WHEN THEY SERVE TOGETHER. HOW COULD YOUR GROUP SERVE SOMEONE IN NEED? YOU MAY WANT TO VISIT A SHUT-IN FROM YOUR CHURCH, PROVIDE A MEAL FOR A FAMILY WHO IS GOING THROUGH DIFFICULTY, OR GIVE SOME OTHER PRACTICAL HELP. IF NOTHING COMES TO MIND, SPEND SOME GROUP TIME PRAYING AND ASKING GOD TO SHOW YOU WHO NEEDS YOUR HELP. THEN HAVE TWO OR THREE GROUP MEMBERS ORGANIZE A SERVING PROJECT FOR THE GROUP, AND DO IT!

5. DEVELOPING OUR ABILITY TO SERVE ACCORDING TO THE LEADING OF THE HOLY SPIRIT TAKES TIME AND PERSISTENCE IN GETTING TO KNOW OUR LORD. SO THE FIRST STEP TOWARD SERVING OTHERS IS, PARADOXICALLY, SPENDING TIME ALONE WITH GOD—PRAYING AND STUDYING AND REFLECTING ON GOD'S WORD. SO WHAT SPECIFIC STEPS WILL YOU TAKE THIS WEEK? IF YOU'VE FOCUSED ON PRAYER IN PAST WEEKS, MAYBE YOU'LL WANT TO DIRECT YOUR ATTENTION TO SCRIPTURE THIS WEEK. IF YOU'VE BEEN READING GOD'S WORD CONSISTENTLY, PERHAPS YOU'LL WANT TO TAKE IT DEEPER AND TRY MEMORIZING A VERSE. TELL THE GROUP WHICH ONE YOU PLAN TO TRY THIS WEEK, AND TALK ABOUT YOUR PROGRESS AND CHALLENGES WHEN YOU MEET NEXT TIME.

6. TO CLOSE THIS SESSION, SPEND SOME TIME WORSHIPPING GOD TOGETHER—PRAYING, SINGING, OR READING SCRIPTURE.

- Have someone use his or her musical gifts to lead the group in a worship song. Try singing a cappella, using a worship CD, or having someone accompany your singing with a musical instrument.

- Choose a psalm or other favorite verse and read it aloud together. Make it a time of praise and worship as the words remind you of all God has done for you.

- Ask, "How can we pray for you this week?" Invite everyone to share, but don't force the issue. Be sure to write prayer requests on your Prayer Requests and Praise Reports on page 87.

- Close your meeting with prayer.

DIGGING DEEPER

TAKE SOME TIME BETWEEN NOW AND OUR NEXT MEETING TO DIG INTO GOD'S WORD. EXPLORE THE BIBLE PASSAGES RELATED TO THIS SESSION'S THEME. JOT DOWN YOUR REFLECTIONS IN A JOURNAL OR IN THIS PARTICIPANT GUIDE. YOU MAY EVEN WANT TO USE A BIBLE WEBSITE OR APP TO LOOK UP COMMENTARY ON THESE PASSAGES. IF YOU LIKE, SHARE WHAT YOU LEARN WITH THE GROUP THE NEXT TIME YOU MEET.

READ LUKE 10:25-37

1. WHY DID THE TEACHER ASK JESUS TO CLARIFY "NEIGHBOR" IN VERSE 29?

2. WHY DID JESUS USE A SAMARITAN AS THE GOOD EXAMPLE IN THIS STORY? HOW WOULD THIS HAVE SHOCKED HIS AUDIENCE?

3. WHAT IS THE SIGNIFICANCE OF OIL AND WINE IN VERSE 34?

4. HOW DOES THE STORY TOLD IN VERSES 30-35 ILLUSTRATE THE "BIG PICTURE" TEACHING OF VERSE 27?

READ 1 PETER 4:10-11

1. HOW IS USING OUR GIFT AN OPPORTUNITY TO ADMINISTER GOD'S GRACE?

2. WHAT PROMISE IS IMPLIED IN VERSE 11 TO THOSE WHO SERVE?

3. WHAT DOES THE END OF THIS PASSAGE REMIND US ABOUT THE ULTIMATE GOAL OF OUR SERVICE?

DAILY DEVOTIONALS

DAY 1 • READ 2 CORINTHIANS 4:5

We don't preach about ourselves. Instead, we preach about Jesus Christ as Lord, and we describe ourselves as your slaves for Jesus' sake (CEB).

RESPOND

It's easy to serve when we get attention and acclaim. What does this verse say we should do instead?

DAY 2 • READ JAMES 4:10

Humble yourselves before the Lord, and he will lift you up (CEB).

RESPOND

Serving others can sometimes be a humbling experience. Sometimes we wrongly feel we're too smart/educated/"together" to do what needs to be done. What does it mean that God will lift us up if we choose to be humble?

DAY 3 • READ MARK 9:35

He sat down, called the Twelve, and said to them, "Whoever wants to be first must be least of all and the servant of all" (CEB).

RESPOND

What does it mean to be the very last? In what way will this make someone "first"?

DAY 4 • READ PHILIPPIANS 2:3-4

Don't do anything for selfish purposes, but with humility think of others as better than yourselves. Instead of each person watching out for their own good, watch out for what is better for others (CEB).

RESPOND

This is difficult! How do you need to consider the good of other people this week? Are there areas of selfishness or conceit you need to confess to God?

DAY 5 • READ 1 CORINTHIANS 15:58

As a result of all this, my loved brothers and sisters, you must stand firm, unshakable, excelling in the work of the Lord as always, because you know that your labor isn't going to be for nothing in the Lord (CEB).

RESPOND

This verse is a great reminder that serving others always matters! Is there a situation in which you need to keep being a servant even though you can't see immediate results? Ask God for his help and wisdom.

DAY 6

Use the following space to write any thoughts God has put in your heart and mind about the things we have looked at in this session and during your Daily Devotions time this week.

_____

_____

_____

FOUND PEOPLE FIND PEOPLE

TODAY WE'RE GOING TO TALK ABOUT WHAT PEOPLE DO AFTER GOD FINDS THEM—THEY FIND OTHERS.

It's probably the most famous, most loved hymn of all time. John Newton wrote "Amazing Grace" after years of involvement in the slave trade. In 1748 he was caught in a violent storm at sea, and his ship was so damaged that he called out to God. A few years later, he finally ended his slave-trading career and began studying the Bible and eventually became an Anglican cleric.

He was lost, and he wrote this song to celebrate being found by God. And today that hymn is sung at churches around the world every weekend. The testimony of his life has affected the lives of millions.

Philip was another person found by God, and today we're going to talk about what people do after God finds them—they find others. Found people find people, and they share the amazing grace of Jesus.

SHARE YOUR STORY

OPEN YOUR GROUP WITH PRAYER. THIS SHOULD BE A BRIEF, SIMPLE PRAYER IN WHICH YOU INVITE GOD TO BE WITH YOU AS YOU MEET. YOU CAN PRAY FOR SPECIFIC REQUESTS AT THE END OF THE MEETING OR STOP MOMENTARILY TO PRAY IF A PARTICULAR SITUATION COMES UP DURING YOUR DISCUSSION.

AS WE HAVE SAID IN PREVIOUS SESSIONS, SHARING OUR PERSONAL STORIES BUILDS DEEPER CONNECTIONS AMONG GROUP MEMBERS. YOUR STORY MAY BE EXACTLY WHAT ANOTHER PERSON NEEDS TO HEAR TO ENCOURAGE OR STRENGTHEN HIM OR HER. AND YOUR LISTENING TO OTHERS' STORIES IS AN ACT OF LOVE AND KINDNESS TO THEM—AND COULD VERY WELL HELP THEM GROW SPIRITUALLY.

BEGIN YOUR TIME TOGETHER BY USING THE FOLLOWING QUESTIONS AND ACTIVITIES TO GET PEOPLE TALKING.

1. HAVE YOU EVER TRIED A RESTAURANT OR SEEN A MOVIE THAT YOU COULDN'T STOP TALKING ABOUT TO OTHER PEOPLE? WHY DID YOU SHARE IT WITH THEM?

2. WHO INTRODUCED YOU TO JESUS?

3. BREAK INTO SMALLER GROUPS AND SHARE YOUR FAITH STORIES.

WATCH
THE DVD

Watch the DVD for this session now. Use the space provided below to record key thoughts, questions, and things you want to remember or follow up on. After you finish watching the video, have someone read the discussion questions in the Hear God's Story section and direct the discussion among the group. As you go through each of the subsequent sections, ask someone else to read the questions and direct the discussion.

_____

_____

_____

_____

_____

_____

_____

HEAR GOD'S STORY

USE THE FOLLOWING QUESTIONS TO GUIDE YOUR DISCUSSION OF THE TEACHING FROM THE VIDEO AND THE BIBLE PASSAGE BELOW.

READ ACTS 8:26-35

An angel from the Lord spoke to Philip, "At noon, take the road that leads from Jerusalem to Gaza." (This is a desert road.) So he did. Meanwhile, an Ethiopian man was on his way home from Jerusalem, where he had come to worship. He was a eunuch and an official responsible for the entire treasury of Candace. (Candace is the title given to the Ethiopian queen.) He was reading the prophet Isaiah while sitting in his carriage. The Spirit told Philip, "Approach this carriage and stay with it."

Running up to the carriage, Philip heard the man reading the prophet Isaiah. He asked, "Do you really understand what you are reading?"

The man replied, "Without someone to guide me, how could I?" Then he invited Philip to climb up and sit with him. This was the passage of scripture he was reading:

Like a sheep he was led to the slaughter
    and like a lamb before its shearer is silent
    so he didn't open his mouth.
In his humiliation justice was taken away from him.
    Who can tell the story of his descendants
        because his life was taken from the earth?

The eunuch asked Philip, "Tell me, about whom does the prophet say this? Is he talking about himself or someone else?" Starting with that passage, Philip proclaimed the good news about Jesus to him (CEB).

1. WHETHER HIS PHYSICAL CONDITION WAS THROUGH CHOICE OR THROUGH BIRTH, THE EUNUCH WOULD HAVE BEEN CONSIDERED "DEFORMED" BY THE JEWISH PEOPLE OF HIS DAY. WHAT IS THE SIGNIFICANCE OF GOD SENDING PHILIP SPECIFICALLY TO FIND THIS PERSON? (LOOK UP DEUTERONOMY 23:1 FOR MORE INSIGHT.)

2. THE SPIRIT ONLY TOLD PHILIP TO GO NEAR THE CHARIOT. WAS IT RIGHT FOR HIM TO STRIKE UP A CONVERSATION?

3. THIS PASSAGE IN ISAIAH WAS (AND IS!) INTERPRETED BY CHRISTIANS AS A PROPHECY ABOUT THE MESSIAH. WHAT KINDS OF THINGS MIGHT PHILIP HAVE POINTED OUT IN THESE VERSES AS A WAY TO TELL THE ETHIOPIAN ABOUT JESUS?

4. HOW IS PHILIP'S EXPERIENCE IN JOHN 1 WITH NATHANAEL SIMILAR TO HIS EXPERIENCE WITH THE ETHIOPIAN?

5. GOD ORCHESTRATED THIS ENTIRE EVENT AND CALLED PHILIP INTO ACTION TO SAVE JUST THIS ONE PERSON. WHAT DOES THIS TELL YOU ABOUT GOD'S LOVE FOR EACH OF US AS INDIVIDUALS?

STUDY NOTES

WE CAN'T KNOW FOR SURE, BUT IT'S LIKELY THE ETHIOPIAN EUNUCH WAS ORIGINALLY A LOWER-CLASS WORKER WHO CHOSE TO BE CASTRATED SO HE COULD WORK IN THE ROYAL COURTS. SOME OF THESE JOBS REQUIRED MEN TO BECOME EUNUCHS SO THEY COULD NEVER FATHER CHILDREN AND POLLUTE THE ROYAL BLOODLINE. THE GREEK WORD, *EUNOUCHOS*, MEANS "BED KEEPER."

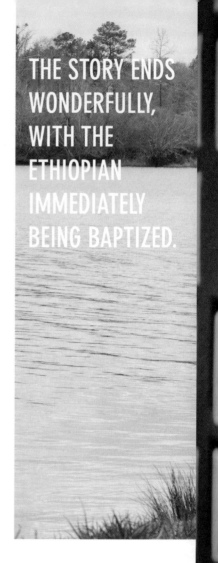

THE STORY ENDS WONDERFULLY, WITH THE ETHIOPIAN IMMEDIATELY BEING BAPTIZED.

SOME SCHOLARS BELIEVE IT'S POSSIBLE THIS MAN HAD GIVEN UP EVERYTHING, INCLUDING THE OPTION OF HAVING HIS OWN FAMILY, SO THAT HE COULD ADVANCE IN HIS CAREER. AND THEN HE LOOKED TO THE JEWISH FAITH FOR MEANING. UNFORTUNATELY, GIVEN HIS PHYSICAL DEFORMITY, HE WOULD LIKELY NOT HAVE BEEN ALLOWED IN THE TEMPLE. NOW, IN ACTS 8, HE'S DOING THE ONLY THING LEFT TO HIM—READING SCRIPTURE (FROM WHAT WOULD HAVE BEEN A VERY EXPENSIVE SCROLL) AND TRYING TO MAKE SENSE OF IT.

CREATE
A NEW
STORY

1. IN THE PASSAGE WE STUDIED, THE ANGEL OF THE LORD AND THE HOLY SPIRIT BOTH PLAYED A KEY ROLE IN HELPING PHILIP "FIND" THE EUNUCH. TODAY WE MAY NOT HEAR AN ANGEL SPEAK, BUT THE SPIRIT STILL HELPS FOUND PEOPLE FIND PEOPLE. HOW CAN YOU HEAR THE SPIRIT'S VOICE IN YOUR LIFE?

2. PHILIP DIDN'T HAVE A CANNED SPEECH OR "TESTIMONY" THAT HE SHARED; HE KNEW THE SCRIPTURES WELL ENOUGH THAT HE COULD START WITH THE EUNUCH'S READING AND GO FROM THERE TO SHARE THE GOSPEL. HOW COMFORTABLE DO YOU FEEL IN EXPLAINING THE BIBLE TO THOSE LESS FAMILIAR WITH IT? HOW MIGHT YOU GROW IN THIS AREA?

3. DO YOU AGREE THAT IT'S A PRIVILEGE TO SHARE JESUS WITH OTHER PEOPLE? OR DOES IT FEEL LIKE A BURDEN? WHY?

4. WHO IN YOUR LIFE NEEDS TO HEAR THE GOOD NEWS OF JESUS? WHO, LIKE THE EUNUCH, MIGHT BE READY AND OPEN TO YOUR WORDS?

5. SPEND SOME TIME PRAYING ABOUT THOSE YOU KNOW WHO MIGHT RESPOND TO A SIMPLE INVITATION: TO COME TO A CHURCH SERVICE, TO JOIN YOUR SMALL GROUP, OR EVEN JUST TO HAVE COFFEE AND TALK ABOUT SPIRITUAL MATTERS. ASK THE HOLY SPIRIT TO BRING TO MIND PEOPLE YOU CAN PRAY FOR.

DIGGING DEEPER

READ MATTHEW 28:18-20

1. THIS PASSAGE, ALSO KNOWN AS THE GREAT COMMISSION, TELLS US TO ACTIVELY SHARE CHRIST WITH THE WORLD. HOW HAVE YOU DONE THAT? WHAT MORE CAN YOU DO?

2. THIS PASSAGE SAYS IT'S NOT ENOUGH TO HELP OTHERS MAKE THE INITIAL CONNECTION TO CHRIST; WE MUST ALSO "DISCIPLE" THEM. WHAT DOES THAT MEAN? HOW DO WE DO IT?

3. WHY WOULD JESUS END THIS COMMISSIONING WITH A PROMISE NOT TO LEAVE US?

READ ROMANS 10:12-15

1. **WHAT DOES IT MEAN TO CALL ON THE NAME OF THE LORD?**

2. **WHAT DOES VERSE 13 TELL US ABOUT OUR RESPONSIBILITY IN BEING FOUND?**

3. **HOW DOES THIS PASSAGE EMPHASIZE THE IMPORTANCE OF OUR EFFORTS TO SHARE JESUS?**

DAILY DEVOTIONALS

DAY 1 • READ PHILEMON 6

I pray that your partnership in the faith might become effective by an understanding of all that is good among us in Christ (CEB).

RESPOND

According to this verse, what is required for us to fully understand our faith?

DAY 2 • READ MATTHEW 9:37-38

Then he said to his disciples, "The size of the harvest is bigger than you can imagine, but there are few workers. Therefore, plead with the Lord of the harvest to send out workers for his harvest" (CEB).

RESPOND

What does Jesus mean when he says the harvest is plentiful? How can you be a worker in the field?

DAY 3 • READ 1 PETER 3:15

Instead, regard Christ as holy in your hearts. Whenever anyone asks you to speak of your hope, be ready to defend it (CEB).

RESPOND

Do you feel prepared in this way? Ask God for insights into how you might grow in this area.

DAY 4 • READ COLOSSIANS 4:5-6

Act wisely toward outsiders, making the most of the opportunity. Your speech should always be gracious and sprinkled with insight so that you may know how to respond to every person (CEB).

RESPOND

What does it mean for your conversation to be "sprinkled with insight"? How can you make the most of the opportunities you have to share Christ?

DAY 5 • READ 2 TIMOTHY 2:15

Make an effort to present yourself to God as a tried-and-true worker, who doesn't need to be ashamed but is one who interprets the message of truth correctly (CEB).

RESPOND

How should we handle God's word?

DAY 6

Use the following space to write any thoughts God has put in your heart and mind about the things we have looked at in this session and during your Daily Devotions time this week.

_____

_____

_____

WORSHIP

IS A

lifestyle

DAVID DANCED AND SANG BEFORE THE LORD.

If you've spent much time in church the last few years, you've probably heard lots of opinions about worship: "The worship music is too loud." "I wish we had more contemporary worship." "I wish we had more traditional worship." "There will be twenty minutes of worship and then a sermon."

We often say "worship" when we mean music, but as we study the life of King David we learn worship is about much more. David danced and sang before the Lord and wrote words we use even now in our praise choruses, but more importantly he consistently strived to please God with his thoughts and his actions. Worship is much more than the songs we sing. It's the lives we lead—lives being transformed by God.

SHARE YOUR STORY

OPEN YOUR GROUP WITH
PRAYER. THIS SHOULD BE
A BRIEF, SIMPLE PRAYER
IN WHICH YOU INVITE GOD
TO BE WITH YOU AS YOU
MEET. YOU CAN PRAY FOR
SPECIFIC REQUESTS AT
THE END OF THE MEETING
OR STOP MOMENTARILY
TO PRAY IF A PARTICULAR
SITUATION COMES UP
DURING YOUR DISCUSSION.

AS WE HAVE SAID IN
PREVIOUS SESSIONS,
SHARING OUR PERSONAL
STORIES BUILDS DEEPER
CONNECTIONS AMONG
GROUP MEMBERS.
YOUR STORY MAY BE
EXACTLY WHAT ANOTHER
PERSON NEEDS TO HEAR
TO ENCOURAGE OR
STRENGTHEN HIM OR HER.
AND YOUR LISTENING TO
OTHERS' STORIES IS AN ACT
OF LOVE AND KINDNESS
TO THEM—AND COULD
VERY WELL HELP THEM
GROW SPIRITUALLY. BEGIN
YOUR TIME TOGETHER BY
USING THE FOLLOWING
QUESTIONS AND ACTIVITIES
TO GET PEOPLE TALKING.

1. WHAT HAS SURPRISED YOU MOST ABOUT THIS GROUP? WHAT HAS GOD TAUGHT YOU IN THESE FIVE WEEKS?

2. DID YOU GROW UP ATTENDING CHURCH? HOW DID THAT EXPERIENCE SHAPE YOUR IDEA OF WHAT WORSHIP IS?

3. HAVE YOU EVER ATTENDED THE WORSHIP SERVICE OF A DIFFERENT FAITH? WHAT WAS THAT EXPERIENCE LIKE?

4. TAKE TIME IN THIS FINAL SESSION TO CONNECT IN SMALLER GROUPS. WHAT HAS GOD BEEN SHOWING YOU THROUGH THESE SESSIONS? WHAT POSITIVE CHANGES HAVE YOU MADE?

5. TAKE SOME TIME FOR EACH PERSON TO SHARE HOW HE OR SHE HAS DONE WITH INVITING PEOPLE TO CHURCH OR YOUR COMMUNITY GROUP. WHAT SPECIFIC CONVERSATIONS ARE YOU PRAYING ABOUT FOR THE WEEKS TO COME?

WATCH
THE DVD

Watch the DVD for this session now. Use the space provided below to record key thoughts, questions, and things you want to remember or follow up on. After you finish watching the video, have someone read the discussion questions in the Hear God's Story section and direct the discussion among the group. As you go through each of the subsequent sections, ask someone else to read the questions and direct the discussion.

HEAR GOD'S STORY

USE THE QUESTIONS ON THE FOLLOWING PAGE TO GUIDE YOUR DISCUSSION OF THE TEACHING FROM THE VIDEO AND THE BIBLE PASSAGE ON THE NEXT PAGE.

READ 2 SAMUEL 6:12-15, 17-18

King David was told, "The LORD has blessed Obed-edom's family and everything he has because of God's chest being there." So David went and brought God's chest up from Obed-edom's house to David's City with celebration. Whenever those bearing the chest advanced six steps, David sacrificed an ox and a fatling calf. David, dressed in a linen priestly vest, danced with all his strength before the LORD. This is how David and the entire house of Israel brought up the LORD's chest with shouts and trumpet blasts. . . .

The LORD's chest was brought in and put in its place inside the tent that David had pitched for it. Then David offered entirely burned offerings in the LORD's presence in addition to well-being sacrifices. When David finished offering the entirely burned offerings and the well-being sacrifices, he blessed the people in the name of the LORD of heavenly forces (CEB).

1. **IT WAS COMMON FOR THERE TO BE RELIGIOUS DANCES AT MOMENTS OF GREAT CELEBRATION, BUT THEY WERE USUALLY ONLY PERFORMED BY THE WOMEN. WHAT ADDITIONAL INSIGHT DOES THIS GIVE US INTO DAVID'S DANCING BEFORE THE LORD?**

2. **WHY MIGHT HE HAVE MADE SACRIFICES AFTER THE PEOPLE CARRYING GOD'S CHEST HAD TAKEN ONLY SIX STEPS?**

3. **THE CHEST WAS SO IMPORTANT BECAUSE IT WAS THE LOCATION OF GOD'S PHYSICAL PRESENCE WITH GOD'S PEOPLE. TODAY, BECAUSE JESUS CAME, WE'RE ALL IN GOD'S PRESENCE CONTINUALLY. HOW DOES THAT AFFECT YOUR THOUGHTS ABOUT WEEKEND WORSHIP AT CHURCH? WHAT ABOUT YOUR DAILY LIVING?**

STUDY NOTES

THE PASSAGE WE STUDIED THIS WEEK INVOLVES DAVID MAKING SACRIFICES AND ENTIRELY BURNED OFFERINGS AS PART OF HIS WORSHIP.

For thousands of years, the Jewish people sacrificed animals, grain, and oil to God in this way. This included killing the animals, pouring out the blood at the base of the altar, cutting the animal into pieces, and then burning the carcass until there was nothing left. This system seems strange to us, but it was how God taught people to worship, and it was normal to them. There were daily sacrifices, sacrifices for specific sins, and sacrifices for festival days.

Of course, this temple sacrifice would inform the great sacrifice that Jesus would make for us on the cross.

CREATE A NEW STORY

1. HOW HAS GOD CHANGED YOUR STORY DURING THIS FIVE-WEEK STUDY? WHAT NEW THINGS IS GOD ASKING YOU TO DO? WHAT TRUTH HAS TRANSFORMED YOUR HEART?

2. THINK ABOUT SPECIFIC STEPS YOU WANT TO TAKE TO LIVE A NEW STORY—TO WALK MORE CLOSELY WITH GOD SO YOU CAN BE PART OF GOD'S STORY?

3. AS YOU WALK FORWARD IN YOUR RELATIONSHIP WITH GOD, WHAT WILL YOU DO DIFFERENTLY AS A RESULT OF WHAT YOU'VE EXPERIENCED IN THIS GROUP?

4. WEEKEND WORSHIP SHOULD JUST BE AN OVERFLOW FROM THE DAILY WAYS WE WORSHIP WITH OUR LIFE. HOW CAN YOU WORSHIP GOD WITH YOUR LIFE THIS WEEK? HOW WILL THAT IMPACT YOUR EXPERIENCE IN CHURCH?

5. WHEN WE WORSHIP, HOW CAN WE MAKE SURE THE FOCUS IS ON GOD, NOT ON US?

6. HOW CAN YOU "GIVE GOD YOUR WHOLE FACE" BY PAYING ATTENTION TO HIM? HOW CAN YOU LOVE HIM BACK?

7. AS THIS IS THE LAST MEETING IN THIS STUDY, TAKE SOME TIME TO CELEBRATE THE WORK GOD HAS DONE IN THE LIVES OF GROUP MEMBERS. HAVE EACH PERSON IN THE GROUP SHARE SOME STEP OF GROWTH HE OR SHE HAS NOTICED IN ANOTHER MEMBER—AFFIRM OTHERS IN THE GROUP. MAKE SURE EACH PERSON GETS AFFIRMED AND NOTICED AND CELEBRATED—WHETHER THE STEPS HE OR SHE HAS MADE ARE LARGE OR SMALL.

8. IF YOUR GROUP STILL NEEDS TO MAKE DECISIONS ABOUT CONTINUING TO MEET AFTER THIS SESSION, HAVE THAT DISCUSSION NOW. TALK ABOUT WHAT YOU WILL STUDY, WHO WILL LEAD, AND WHERE AND WHEN YOU WILL MEET.

9. REVIEW YOUR COMMUNITY GROUP COVENANT ON PAGE 83 AND EVALUATE HOW WELL YOU MET YOUR GOALS. DISCUSS ANY CHANGES YOU WANT TO MAKE AS YOU MOVE FORWARD. IF YOU PLAN TO CONTINUE MEETING, AND YOUR GROUP STARTS A NEW STUDY, THIS IS A GREAT TIME TO TAKE ON A NEW ROLE OR CHANGE ROLES OF SERVICE IN YOUR GROUP. WHAT NEW ROLE WILL YOU TAKE ON? IF YOU ARE UNCERTAIN, MAYBE SOMEONE WOULD LIKE TO SHARE THE ROLE WITH YOU IF YOU DON'T FEEL READY TO SERVE SOLO.

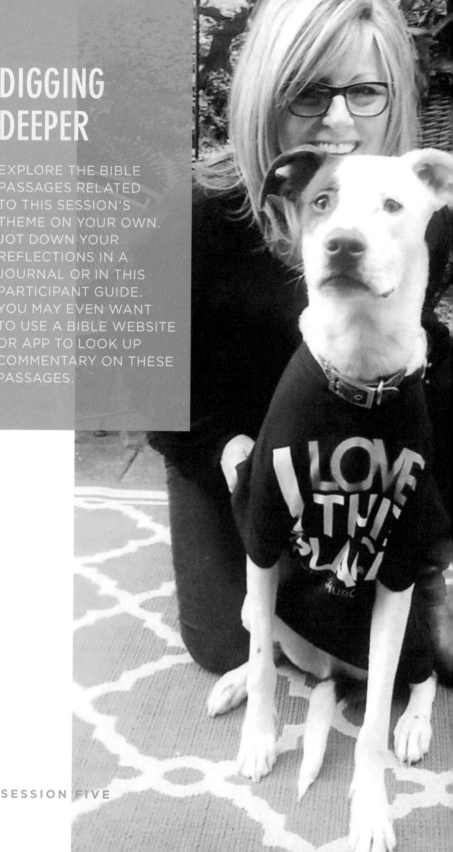

DIGGING DEEPER

EXPLORE THE BIBLE PASSAGES RELATED TO THIS SESSION'S THEME ON YOUR OWN. JOT DOWN YOUR REFLECTIONS IN A JOURNAL OR IN THIS PARTICIPANT GUIDE. YOU MAY EVEN WANT TO USE A BIBLE WEBSITE OR APP TO LOOK UP COMMENTARY ON THESE PASSAGES.

READ MATTHEW 22:37-40

1. **WHY IS THIS CONSIDERED THE GREATEST COMMANDMENT?**

2. **WHAT DOES IT MEAN THAT "ALL THE LAW AND THE PROPHETS DEPEND ON THESE TWO COMMANDS"?**

3. **THESE COMMANDMENTS BEGIN WITH THE WORD *LOVE* INSTEAD OF *DO* OR *SAY* OR *OBEY*. WHAT IS THE SIGNIFICANCE OF THIS?**

READ JOHN 4:23-24

1. WHAT DOES IT MEAN TO WORSHIP "IN SPIRIT AND TRUTH"?

2. WHAT DOES THIS VERSE HAVE TO SAY TO THOSE WHO THINK WORSHIP MUST INVOLVE A CERTAIN BUILDING/STYLE/SONG/COLLECTION OF WORDS?

3. DOES IT SURPRISE YOU TO READ THAT THE FATHER SEEKS WORSHIPPERS?

DAILY DEVOTIONALS

DAY 1 • READ COLOSSIANS 3:16

The word of Christ must live in you richly. Teach and warn each other with all wisdom by singing psalms, hymns, and spiritual songs. Sing to God with gratitude in your hearts (CEB).

RESPOND

Thankfulness is consistently linked to worship. How can the "richness" of Christ fill your life today? What part of his message are you thankful for?

DAY 2 • READ PSALM 40:3

He put a new song in my mouth, / a song of praise for our God. / Many people will learn of this and be amazed; / they will trust the Lord (CEB).

RESPOND

According to this verse, what is a benefit of praising God in addition to our own relationship with Him?

DAY 3 • READ ROMANS 12:1

So, brothers and sisters, because of God's mercies, I encourage you to present your bodies as a living sacrifice that is holy and pleasing to God. This is your appropriate priestly service (CEB).

RESPOND

What does it mean to be a living sacrifice? How can we be holy and pleasing to God?

DAY 4 • READ PSALM 95:6-7

Come, let's worship and bow down! / Let's kneel before the Lord, our maker! / He is our God, / and we are the people of his pasture, / the sheep in his hands (CEB).

RESPOND

Kneeling is a common posture for worship throughout the ages, often meant to signify respect for God. Take a few minutes today to kneel right where you are and thank him for being your creator and shepherd.

DAY 5 • READ REVELATION 5:13

And I heard every creature in heaven and on earth and under the earth and in the sea—I heard everything everywhere say, "Blessing, honor, glory, and power belong / to the one seated on the throne / and to the Lamb / forever and always" (CEB).

RESPOND

Someday we will worship God constantly as we live in God's presence for eternity. Today, thank God for God's faithfulness to you and praise God for your salvation!

DAY 6

Use the following space to write any thoughts God has put in your heart and mind about the things we have looked at in this session and during your Daily Devotions time this week.

_____

_____

_____

APPENDICES

RESOURCES TO MAKE YOUR SMALL GROUP
EXPERIENCE EVEN BETTER!

FREQUENT QUESTIONS

WHAT DO WE DO AT OUR FIRST COMMUNITY GROUP MEETING?

Have a party! Make it fun. A "get to know you" coffee, meal, or dessert is a great way to launch a new study. You may want to review the Community Group Covenant (page 83), and discuss the names of a few friends you can invite to join your group. Don't jump right into study time. Get to know each other first. Even if you are already close, talk about something that happened that week.

WHERE DO WE FIND NEW PARTICIPANTS FOR OUR COMMUNITY GROUP?

Adding people to a group can be troubling. We get comfortable with each other, and then find it awkward to bring in another relationship. Even new groups of four or five people can sense this intimacy. And groups of friends who have been together will lose a few people but not think to recruit new participants. After your group prays about their purpose, create together a list of people to welcome from your neighborhood, your workplaces, your children's school, your families, the gym, and so on. Each participant would then invite the people on his or her list. Church leaders are also willing to announce that your community group is open and welcoming, or put the list of groups in a bulletin insert.

It's very healthy to remain open and welcoming so that new participants can join your group. Attrition happens in groups as people move to new locations, or take on new leadership roles, or hear the calling into other ministry opportunities. So before the group becomes small, making it at risk of stopping, stay open—God will send interesting people your way. You might meet your best friend forever.

HOW LONG WILL COMMUNITY GROUPS MEET?

Most community groups meet weekly for at least their first five weeks. Every other week can work too. In the early months, try to meet weekly as

a group. When life happens or when a job requires someone to miss a meeting, they won't miss a month if the group meets occasionally.

At the end of this community group study, each group member may choose whether to stay in the community group or look for another study. Some groups launch relationships that last many years, and others are temporary signposts on the journey into another group experience. The journey is what matters.

CAN WE DO THIS STUDY ON OUR OWN?

One of the best ways to do this study is not with a full house but with a few friends, coworkers, or neighbors. You may prefer to gather with another couple to walk through this study. Then you can be flexible about other ways to grow deeper in friendship by going to see a movie or going out for dinner. God's spirit is present even when two or three are seeking guidance through the scriptures and in prayer (Matt 18:20).

WHAT IF THIS GROUP IS NOT WORKING FOR US?

Sometimes a group encounters a personality conflict, life-stage difference, geographical distance, varied levels of spiritual maturity, or many other differences. Take a breath and pray for God's guidance. When this five-week study is complete, decide whether your group is a good fit for you. It often takes eight to nine weeks for a small group to bond and appreciate each other, so don't bail

out before the five weeks of this study are up—God might have something to teach you. Also, don't run from conflict or prejudge a person or group before you have given them a chance. Have you ever noticed that as soon as a difficult person leaves a group, someone else in the group will take their place! God is still working in your life too!

WHO IS THE LEADER?
Healthy community groups rotate hosts/leaders and homes on a regular basis. By sharing the leadership or hosting, participants can learn their unique gifts and feel satisfaction from their contribution. This study guide and the Holy Spirit can keep things on track even when you rotate discussion leaders. Christ promised to be in your midst when you gather. Ultimately, God is your leader each step of the way.

HOW DO WE HANDLE THE CHILD CARE NEEDS IN OUR GROUP?
Handle child care with sensitive thinking. Ask the group to openly suggest solutions. If one approach does not work, adjust to another. Many groups share the cost of a babysitter (or two), who can watch the kids in a different part of the house or yard. Another option is to use one home for the kids and a second home (close by or a phone call away) for the adults. Or if the group has enough adults, the responsibility can be rotated among the adults for the children, either in the same home or in another home nearby. Kids respond well when they see how other parents care for them. Of course, typically each parent can make their own arrangements for their children. Speak openly with each other about the responsibility and the resolution.

COMMUNITY GROUP COVENANT

OUR PURPOSE
To provide a predictable environment where participants experience authentic community and spiritual growth.

OUR GROUP EXPECTATIONS

Showing Up
We will make an effort through our presence in each group meeting. We will call or e-mail if we cannot attend or will arrive late. (If the Group Calendar is completed, participants will know when to meet.)

Comfortable Environment
Participants will be heard and feel loved. They will know this because we listen to each other's answers and judgments with respect. Our replies will be gentle and gracious because we are at different stages of spiritual maturity, and our "imperfections" indicate where we are each under construction, moving on toward a complete and whole life together.

Keeping Secrets
When participants share private and intimate aspects of their personal life, we will not share this outside the group, and we will avoid gossiping about others outside the group.

Healthy Growth
Participants will serve others with their God-given gifts, and they will help others in the group to discover their own strengths and gifts.

Everyone in Ministry
Every participant will take on a role or responsibility over time in the group.

Rotating Hosts and Homes
Each participant is encouraged to host the group in his or her home and rotate the responsibility of facilitating a meeting. (See the Group Calendar on page 85.)

COMMUNITY GROUP CALENDAR

Chart out the details together!

Date	Lesson	Host Home	Dessert/Meal	Leader
	1			
	2			
	3			
	4			
	5			

Group Project:

Group Social:

COMMUNITY GROUP ROSTER

Name	Phone	E-mail

PRAYER REQUESTS AND PRAISE REPORTS

	Prayer Requests	Praise Reports	
Session 1			Session 1
Session 2			Session 2
Session 3			Session 3
Session 4			Session 4
Session 5			Session 5

MEMORY VERSES CLIP AND REVIEW

SESSION ONE
Don't stop meeting together with other believers, which some people have gotten into the habit of doing. Instead, encourage each other, especially as you see the day drawing near. (Heb 10:25 CEB)

SESSION TWO
Instead, like a newborn baby, desire the pure milk of the word. Nourished by it, you will grow into salvation, since you have tasted that the Lord is good. (1 Pet 2:2-3 CEB)

SESSION THREE
"In everything I have shown you that, by working hard, we must help the weak. In this way we remember the Lord Jesus' words: 'It is more blessed to give than to receive.'" (Acts 20:35 CEB)

SESSION FOUR
The fruit of the righteous is a tree of life, / and the wise gather lives. (Prov 11:30 CEB)

SESSION FIVE
My mouth is filled with your praise, / glorifying you all day long. (Ps 71:8 CEB)

CLIP AND
REVIEW THE
MEMORY VERSES
ON THE OTHER
SIDE OF THIS
PAGE.

COMMUNITY GROUP LEADERS

Key resources to help your leadership experience be the best it can be

STARTING A NEW COMMUNITY GROUP

New community groups can often grow and multiply because the participants gather with more openness than existing small groups. An "open house" is a particularly good way to meet and break the ice with each other before the first session of a group study. The group can also discuss other persons to invite as the study begins. Discuss what each participant can expect from the group, and start off the right way by praying briefly for each other.

In the Gospels, especially in Matthew and Luke, food around a table with teaching is often in the mix when the disciples and seekers are engaged in learning and growing spiritually. So when launching a new community group, tasty desserts or a basic meal will probably stimulate the joy of doing life together.

Ask the participants to introduce themselves and share how or why they are present in this group. If the participants seem shy, you can ask some leading questions:

· What is the most memorable experience from a vacation?
· What is one thing that you appreciate about your community, town, or city?
· Describe a couple things about your childhood that the participants would not know.

Review the Community Group Covenant and talk about each person's expectations and priorities.

Finally, place an empty seat or two in the middle of your group and encourage the group participants to think about a person who could fill that chair or seat over the next few weeks. Provide postcards and have each participant complete one or two invitations. If you get more people than can fit in a room, split into two rooms for discussion. If more than one discussion group is engaged, at the end of a weekly session, gather the whole group for prayer and sharing something they appreciated about the meeting.

While a kick-off meeting might be skipped by an established or experienced small group, any group will experience awakening and renewal by focusing on the purposes of an outwardly focused community group.

LEADING OR HOSTING A DISCUSSION

- If you are nervous about leading a group discussion, you are a healthy and humble person. God usually speaks through reluctant and ordinary persons. God is already present, working ahead in each life through the means of grace (such as personal prayer or searching the scriptures).

- You have gifts that no one else has in the group. So be yourself and listen. Try to limit your talking time to 20 percent of the discussion so that other participants do 80 percent of the talking.

- You are not alone. Other leaders or good friends can pray for you and prepare with you before the discussion.

- Be ready. Go through the session several times. Listen to the teaching segment for the session on the DVD. Write notes in a Bible or in a journal to listen for what God would speak through you. Don't procrastinate. Prepare before the meeting.

- Get evaluation from the participants. Ask them to send an e-mail or write on cards at the meeting about two or three things they liked from the discussion and one thing that could be improved. Be humble and open to growing as a leader or host.

- Tell your group how this study or group relationships are helping you, personally, draw closer to God and friends. Share your struggles and blessings. Others will see your example and can relate with their own lives.

- Carefully consider another person whom you will ask to lead the group discussion next week. Ask in person, without putting someone on the spot. This is one of the benefits of a community group. The leaders and participants are the same, not experts, because they can't do life alone either.

10 HOST TIPS

1. Relax! Now, breathe! You can do this, and we're here to help if you get stuck. Remember, God is with you. Pray up, prepare, and be friendly. You can do this! Read Hebrews 13:5.

2. Invite. Now invite some more people to join you for this short five week journey. You are the key to filling your group. #foundpeoplefindpeople

3. Serve a few snacks. Food helps break the ice. Keep it simple and then share this responsibility weekly with your group members.

4. Prepare for your time together. Preview the DVD, write down your thoughts, and select questions that you feel will work best in your group. #growingpeoplechange

5. Pray for your group members. Follow up with them during the week about the concerns in their lives. Make prayer and reaching out to God a regular part of group life. #worshipisalifestyle

6. Maintain a healthy atmosphere. Don't allow anyone, including yourself, to dominate discussion or fall into gossip. Redirect gently when conversation deviates.

7. Be prepared for questions. As questions arise don't feel like you have to know all the answers. Just say, "I don't know. Let me check that out." Then contact the church office for some help.

8. Allow silence. When you ask questions, if there is silence for a moment, don't jump in too quickly to rescue. This may just be a sign that people are thoughtful about how to respond.

9. Tackle a mission project together! How can you and your group make a difference in the world? Do it! We'd love to hear your stories about it and see pictures! #savedpeopleservepeople

10. Have fun! Plan to do something in this five week time outside of the group time together just for fun. It helps build friendships and makes the journey more fun together! #youcan'tdolifealone